Glorifying God

at the

Rocks of Remembrance

Dr. Emily Grace Hervey

Glorifying God at the Rocks of Remembrance

Cover designed by Rob Grant and Emily Hervey

Published by
Worldwide Writings, LLC

www.worldwidewritings.com

Blessed are those whose strength is in you,
who have set their hearts on pilgrimage.
As they pass through the Valley of Baca,
they make it a place of springs;
the autumn rains also cover it with pools.
They go from strength to strength,
till each appears before God in Zion.
(Psalm 84: 5-7)

Table of Contents

Introduction

I'm done! These words kept going through my mind on the cool May morning in southeastern Washington. Around me many other graduating seniors exchanged greetings with a congratulatory attitude, holding at the same time the bittersweet undertone of approaching farewells. As the grey, sprinkling clouds threatened more rain, our black graduation gowns and caps served as convenient coverings.

After four years in college, we adopted an official group title: the Class of 2007. In our matching garments we were squeezed into the width of the camera's lens for our group photo, then were directed to form alphabetical lines, eventually progressing into the rows of seats reserved solely for us. The various microphoned statements spoke to us almost as a single entity. And for once, I did actually seem to fit the requirements of being considered part of the larger group, one of the soon-to-be alumni.

Lakum Duckum: A place for thinking, drawing, reading, and even watching other students play Frisbee golf.

Like everyone else I'd successfully completed my coursework, passed my exams, written and presented my thesis. I'd lived in a dorm, eaten in the cafeteria, spent late nights in the library, noticed the colorful leaves in the fall, seen our central field frosted in the winter, and witnessed the annual spring proliferation of ducklings around our pond and streams. We all had our memories, the stories to tell about experiences on and off campus, the exciting and grueling classes, the events, debates, clubs, activities, and traditions; the interactions with professors, peers, and staff members. And we had all reached the end point of that chapter of life.

At the same time, each one of us held a unique perspective and our experiences spread across a wide spectrum. The question of *"What's next?"* prompted a variety of answers, ranging from specified goals to vague plans that held uncertainties about the future. We came from diverse backgrounds and were headed in distinct directions. Somehow I felt I had trekked an atypical path, one with many bumps in the road, unexpected turns, rough terrain, steep mountains, and deep valleys. To me, graduation held great significance after going through periods when I wasn't sure I'd make it this far.

On my journey I had learned that some steps along the way I could not take by myself, but instead had to turn to a greater source of strength: the loving grace of my Sovereign Lord. Many people before me have faced far more than I have, but I want to do what the Israelites did after many years trekking through the wilderness. When they finally crossed the Jordan River after forty years in the desert, the first thing they did was to build a memorial of twelve stones, a place where they could remember to pass on lessons taken from all God had done to guide and sustain them.

They did not build it to show their own endurance and accomplishments; instead it was a reminder that boundaries were crossed solely when led by the presence and grace of God, as represented in the Ark of the Covenant (Joshua 4:7). Can you imagine that sense of amazement and fulfillment, as the overwhelming floods of Jordan River water were supernaturally held back, that final barrier crossed, the promise given hundreds of years earlier ultimately fulfilled? The Israelites had to go through a long process of learning before being prepared to cross that river and face further battles; they had to learn to trust fully in God. But He fulfilled His promise and didn't want them to

Twelve stones were erected as a remembrance of all God had done to bring His people to the Promised Land.

forget His faithfulness. So they took twelve stones and created an altar of remembrance.

My journey is on a much smaller scale than that of Israel, but I too want to remember what I have learned over the course of several years, in the midst of unexpected transitions and uncertainties about my health. My Lord has shown me more about Himself through my own desert wanderings. I have had the chance to witness His loving faithfulness, in the midst of challenging circumstances. I am continually amazed by His all-encompassing sovereignty. His ultimately glorious nature is central to His lordship, and yet His amazing grace is always available.

God has allowed me to face my own questions about the reason for suffering. I have discovered more about the importance of trust, closely related to the need to surrender. In the midst of these questions, the motivation to rejoice is also growing. He has shown me ways I can take part in His plan, even the midst of challenges. Part of this comes through the overflow of His comfort. He has power as our Creator to use us, and even more amazingly, He transforms our weaknesses through His glorious strength. Finally, His incredible plan is filled with opportunities to accept and share

His gift of love. These themes make up my twelve stones, which I divided into four sections, each holding three areas of learning. Just as the Israelites set up the twelve rocks on their altar, I pray my altar of remembrance will likewise be glorifying to God.

Learning about:

My Lord	Faithfulness	Sovereignty	Glory	Grace
Myself	Suffering	Trust	Surrender	Rejoice
My Place in His Plan	Overflowing Comfort	In the Potter's Hands	Strength in Weakness	Sharing Love

Our God is Faithful

Statements such as "God is loving," and "God is faithful," are easy to say in the "happy" times of life, when we have no reason to question such propositions. But in such an environment those words can appear shallow. What makes Him faithful? Where do you see His love? How do you know the depth of that faithful love? God's faithfulness is most needed and most evident in the painful times of life, the uncertainties and fears, the grief and feelings of abandonment. I've learned this through experience, through years of uncertainty, struggling with both what was going on around me and what was happening in my own body. There were moments of despair, and moments of encountering God out of my own necessity for His comfort.

I spent my childhood on three different continents, moving from the windy tip of South America, to the Westernized culture of Southern California, then on to the steppes of

Central Asia. Changes and cultural adjustments became the norm, home became a relative term, and "fitting in" seemed outside my reach. When arriving as the only American family in a small city by the Caspian Sea, I felt isolated and my pillow absorbed many a tear. But in that context God's faithfulness and consistency became ever more real and comforting. I could always depend on His Presence, His Love, His Sovereignty.

Over and over in the psalms the writer will praise God's faithfulness just a few words after lamenting in the midst of incredible difficulty. Many of the psalms were written by David, a man who endured many overwhelming circumstances of danger, betrayal, and rejection. On one occasion David cried out,

"The arrogant are attacking me, O God; a band of ruthless men seeks my life—men without regard for you. But you, O Lord, are a compassionate and gracious God, slow to anger, abounding in love and faithfulness. Turn to me and have mercy on me; grant your strength to your servant and save the son of your maidservant. Give me a sign of your goodness, that my enemies may see it and be put to shame, for you, O Lord, have

helped me and comforted me." (Psalm 86: 14-17)

It takes faith to recognize God's faithfulness in the midst of those dark valleys; it is often when we have nowhere else to turn that we realize our need for His unfailing love. Over and over David was attacked, outnumbered, threatened, and unable to endure such opposition by his own human capacities. His psalms often reflected how crushed he felt, yet he repeatedly recognized the power of God and his need to rely on God's faithfulness. He must have felt at his wit's end when asking for mercy and strength.

We know the complete version of David's story, including many victories and a successful reign. But imagine what it would've been like in thick of it, when facing a giant, when being rejected by the king he served, when fleeing for his life, and when greatly outnumbered. Many questions could have been going through his mind: "Why is God allowing this to happen to me, after all the promises He gave me? Why did He choose me, a shepherd boy, to be in this position? What happened to His promises of reigning over a kingdom?" Perhaps he even had feelings of doubt and regret. Life would have been much simpler and safer as a shepherd.

Instead he was in a place of little control and overwhelming odds. Yet David clung to God's faithfulness, which carried him to victory.

David was not the only person in the Bible who called out to God in the unbearable circumstances. Lamentations is a well-named book of the Bible: the author, most likely Jeremiah, is almost constantly mourning. The original Hebrew title of the book is *'ekah*, which means "How...!" Isn't that the question or expression of desperation we feel in times of sorrow? How could this be happening? How will I get through it? The poetical book was written during a time of very little hope, as Israelites had no way to understand why God allowed the destruction of Jerusalem and the expulsion of Jews from their country, the Promised Land God had once given to them. Yet, despite these unanswered questions, in the third chapter the writer is still grasping for hope (vs. 19-32):

*"I remember my affliction and my wandering, the bitterness and the gall. I well remember them, and my soul is downcast within me. Yet this I call to mind and therefore I have **hope**: Because of the Lord's great love we are not consumed, for his compassions never fail. They are new every morning; great is your **faithfulness**. I*

say to myself, 'The Lord is my portion;
therefore I will wait for him.' The Lord is
good to those whose **hope** *is in him, to the*
one who seeks him; it is good to wait quietly
for the salvation of the Lord. It is good for a
man to bear the yoke while he is young. Let
him sit alone in silence, for the Lord has
laid it on him. Let him bury his face in the
dust-- there may yet be **hope**. *Let him offer*
his cheek to one who would strike him, and
let him be filled with disgrace. For men are
not cast off by the Lord forever. Though he
brings grief, he will show compassion, so
great is his unfailing love" (emphasis
added).

Even though His people turned their backs on Him, God did not forever turn His back on His people. When reading the passage in Lamentations it seems to suggest that God is the source of suffering when reading words such as "disgrace," "cast off," and "grief." How do these fit with the promise of compassion, faithfulness, and love? When reading the historical events, there is a cyclical pattern of God's people enjoying the easy life, slipping away from God, and not turning back to Him until He has allowed them suffering.

Why Suffering?

While initially we might see God as a tyrant for the destruction He brought to Israel, I think we should be amazed that He did not simply give up on His people. Instead, He did what was necessary to turn them back to Him, actions coming from His love. This love culminated in His gift of salvation through Christ, who took all suffering upon Himself.

Because of that gift, today we don't have to be part of a political nation to be His people. Nor do we need priests as intermediaries between us and God. We have direct access to grace and forgiveness through Christ. But we still live in a fallen world, which has two negative consequences. First, we can easily see our own selfishness subtly pulling us away from God. At times it takes disaster to pull us back to Him. In this case, suffering may be a gift significant on an eternal level. But this does not mean that all suffering is a result of our misdeeds or a form of punishment.

The second consequence of being in a fallen world is that Satan still has some authority, and without the complete rule of Christ, bad things happen. Throughout history and across the globe many have struggled with the question: "If there is a good and loving God, then why is there so much suffering all around us?" That question trails everything from natural disasters to human-made tragedies, from widespread epidemics to an individual's physical pain, from political uproar to disputes within one's own family. It often accompanies a sense of doubt in oneself and in God. Where is God's love in that tragedy? If God were faithful, why didn't He stop this persecution? What is amazing is that God can use even those tragedies for good. In fact, suffering is what often allows us to encounter God's faithfulness. Psalm 91 says:

"He who dwells in the shelter of the Most High will rest in the shadow of the Almighty. I will say of the Lord, 'He is my refuge and my fortress, my God, in whom I trust.' Surely he will save you from the fowler's snare and from the deadly pestilence. He will cover you with his

feathers, and under his wings you will find refuge; his faithfulness will be your shield and rampart" (vs. 1-4).

Just as expressed in this passage, periods of affliction can allow us to experience His faithfulness. He does not forget us, even when we can't understand why He allows something to happen. In fact, His faithfulness would mean little to nothing without hardships, simply because we wouldn't need it! This passage reminds of the need to wait. We can't expect an immediate understanding of all our troubles, but we can still hold on to hope. Knowing God as faithful is a promise when we reach rock bottom, when we need shelter from a storm, or when feel utterly alone.

There have been a number of times when I too struggled with the "why" question. While I was growing up, my family moved from Chile, where I was born, to California for two years, then off to Central Asia. Although young, I was aware to some degree that these transitions were for the purpose of following God's calling. After arriving in Kazakhstan, my family spent three years of investing in the lives around us, running a non-profit educational center to teach English and computers to eager learners, and sharing the hope that we had in Christ with those who were searching for truth.

Some aspects of that time were very difficult for me, particularly struggling with language learning, loneliness, and at times feeling like I had no significant role there. Yet, at the same time I learned so much through experience and developed close friendships with other foreigners who worked with us, the Team. We worshiped God together, celebrated holidays together, prayed together, and watched God's hand at work together. I always looked forward to Friday nights, when our team would gather for four hours of teaching, worship, prayer, and food.

After three years spent in this city, my family took a year-long furlough in California. Upon return I stepped into the "oldest sister" role, as both my older sisters stayed in the US. During my parents' trip in January, that bled into the position of "substitute mom," as I took on more of the household responsibilities. Soon after my parents' return, our team faced some opposition from the local government, as the Vice Governor ordered an investigation of our organization. It appeared more like a search for evidence to count against us. One Sunday in February police came to the kindergarten where a weekly service was held, led mostly by local believers. They filmed the service, and later that a team-member playing guitar was exhibiting "religious leadership," which was not permitted under our visas. Police also interrogated and threatened numerous people, including my father. At the educational center they demanded to see files, and soon after made it impossible to rent the building being used.

In the midst of searching for a new building to use for our educational center and attempting to comply with any statements of required changes from the government, we heard nothing about the result of the investigation. It looked like it had blown over; perhaps they couldn't find enough evidence to use against us. My parents were considering going to a conference in England and wanted more clarity on the status of the investigation. When my father approached the officials in charge of the investigation, he was told the report would be favorable.

With that reassurance and the previous positive experience of running the house in January, I gave my approval for the trip. I had the help of another young woman who was in town for a year, allowing me the time to continue my own studies. Soon after they left, I received a phone call from another person on the team. *We got a call from the government...we're going to have a team meeting tomorrow.* At age fourteen I was certainly the youngest at the meeting, but was in many ways grateful to be included. When I heard the news that the local government wanted to take the case to court in order to get us expelled from the country, my first concern was whether my parents would be able to get back from England. But with the government's intent to get the black stamp on the passports that would keep us out permanently, that was not a problem. My father needed to be in town for the trial.

The following month was full of twists and turns that at times seemed surreal. It was unclear how quickly the process would go, and how likely it was to win a case in a corrupt judiciary system. One day we thought our case (or subsequent appeals to a higher authority that would follow the judge's expected decision) could serve as a precursor for similar cases. Thus it could be important to fight it out to the end. The next day input from a local lawyer left us making plans of how to escape from the country with "clean" passports. *Should we try to take a train to a different border? Is it still too cold for there to be a ferry across the Caspian Sea? If by air, we'll need to go in two groups...*

As we vacillated between options, my father often left the apartment to avoid court summons when officials came pounding at our door. Finally, the team decided to try to leave by air. The first group made it on a flight across the Caspian, despite a government officer's attempted claim of authority to detain them. But when the three remaining families got to the airport in the wee hours of that March morning, we were stopped. After hours in a cold cement airport, a signature from a higher official declared that only the women and children could depart. We all stayed together, rather than leaving just the men.

I fell asleep upon arriving back at the apartment that morning, only to be awakened by a phone call in Russian from the police, which in my confused state I passed on to my father. Later that day officials again came to our door, court summons in hand. The trial was scheduled for Good Friday, the day we remember Christ standing trial and being condemned despite his innocence. Although the trial was postponed until the day after Easter, I reflected that weekend on Christ's sufferings from a very different angle. Was I getting a tiny taste of his grief when facing rejection and condemnation from the very people he had come to serve and teach? At the same time, considering the incredible anguish he endured when taking on the world's sins and being separated from God, put our own challenge in perspective; it was nothing compared to his suffering. And even in the midst of not knowing what was ahead, we had reason to celebrate Christ's victory.

That Monday my parents left in the morning, my father reporting to the court room and my mother picking up a US consulate at the airport on the way. I waited tentatively all morning, trying to distract myself with my own studies. The phone rang at 1PM: *The trial is over, now we're just waiting for the judge's decision.* Several more hours crept by, longer than expected when assuming the verdict was passed before the trial began. Then the news came that the ruling was against us, charging major fines and giving us ten days to leave the country. A week in the chaos of packing followed, seeing visitors with the awareness we might never meet again, a gathering on my birthday that was more a goodbye party.

On my father's birthday we were back at the airport. Officials seemed to be trying to make it hard for us, unzipping every bag and unwrapping packed birthday presents. The TV news cameras recorded our shameful exodus with no positive coverage.

It was hard to believe we were actually leaving permanently when staring out the plane window.

Then it was over. We were on the plane, leaving permanently. It was as if that chapter of life was not just closed, but slammed shut. *Is this what we get after years of serving them?*

Arriving back to the US allowed the adrenaline of the roller coaster slow down, and the painful emotions set in. We were greeted by well-meaning friends welcoming us "home" and stating how glad we must be to get out of there. I had just lost my home and found myself in a completely different context where no one around me could relate to my experience. All norms had disappeared and our team members were no longer next door. I attempted to bury myself in the remainder of my school work, a convenient distraction. Yet underneath the questions still nagged me: *Why did you let this happen, God? Weren't we doing your work? Weren't we helping them?*

Comfort Overflows

It wasn't until a couple months later that our whole team was able to regroup in the dry heat of Arizona for a time of de-briefing and a retreat. Simply being with those who had a common experience, a mutual understanding, and a similar perspective was refreshing. Together sharing and processing the past events served as salve to a wound. It was during that time that God gave me a passage from 2nd Corinthians where Paul wrote:

"Praise be to the God and Father of our Lord Jesus Christ, the Father of compassion and the God of all comfort, who comforts us in all our troubles, so that we can comfort those in any trouble with the comfort we ourselves have received from God. For just as the sufferings of Christ flow over into our lives, so also through Christ our comfort overflows. If we are distressed, it is for your comfort and salvation; if we are comforted,

it is for your comfort, which produces in you patient endurance of the same sufferings we suffer" (2nd Corinthians 1:3-6).

These verses resonated for me, partly because God had already been planting in me a desire to serve others through a career in psychology or counseling, more specifically, providing care for missionaries. I realized that what I had just experienced would allow me to look into the lives of others who also faced suffering in the context of serving God, laying down their lives for His kingdom. Now I could understand on a much deeper level the rejection, pain, disappointment, fear, uncertainty, and grief so often endured.

But it was not only my ability to help others that was being honed; it was the chance to actually experience and receive Christ's comfort, the never-ending, always available flow of loving compassion. This comfort comes from the one who willfully chose to become human and endured far more than we could even imagine. He is not an aloof deity whose sympathy is superficial. The deep empathy He offers is what we too can pass on to others. Allowing God's loving comfort to overflow from my life would be far more powerful and effective than trying to create my own comfort to offer others. And when we look at how the verse starts, we see that the opportunity to experience and pass on the Father's compassion is a reason to praise Him, the one whose incredible love led to ultimate sacrifice for our sake.

In this passage, and several others in the New Testament, the presence of suffering was not questioned, it was assumed! When the church that began two thousand years ago faced constant opposition and persecution they accepted it joyfully. In fact, it served as confirmation that they were on the right track, following the very footsteps of Christ. In one of his letters Peter writes,

"Dear friends, do not be surprised at the painful trial you are suffering, as though something strange were happening to you. But rejoice that you participate in the sufferings of Christ, so that you may be overjoyed when his glory is revealed. If you are insulted because of the name of Christ, you are blessed, for the Spirit of glory and of God rests on you" (1 Peter 4: 12-14).

Accepting and following Christ was a package deal, with suffering and rejoicing coming hand in hand. If there is a desire to draw near to Christ, how can one turn down the chance to experience a piece of His expression of love to the human race through suffering? Of course our natural human tendencies balk at the prospect; we far prefer the appealing opportunity of participating in the miraculous and restorative components of His ministry. But were His miracles the primary reason for coming to earth? Or did His salvation through death on the cross outweigh those events?

Fortunately the story did not end there, and our participation is not only in His suffering. His resurrection and glorification for eternity far surpassed the finite experience of pain. We have the overarching promise and hope of participating in His glory for eternity, a blessing so far out of our ability to conceptualize that we easily forget to take it into account in the midst of current trials.

After being expelled from Kazakhstan, I had a number of conversations with other Christians in the United States who, upon hearing my story, acted rather appalled. How could such a thing happen living in what is supposed to be a free world? It felt as though many Americans were oblivious to what is happening daily across the globe. Persecution is very real, and believers are constantly being denounced, imprisoned, and martyred. In that setting, willingness to follow Christ is synonymous with readiness for suffering. You had better have a good reason to call yourself a believer, and must be able to trust in God's faithfulness during the assumed trials ahead.

In the US, there appears to be a lot more room for ambiguity: people can call themselves Christians or say they believe in Christ, yet not live it out on a daily basis. Most are not forced to evaluate their allegiance at the possible cost of death. Even those who do truly believe in God may be hesitant to declare Christ as the ultimate truth, for fear of others looking down on them.

I easily slip into that frame of mind, avoiding confrontation to prevent offending others, which could easily lead to rejection. While I would stand by my faith if challenged, proactively seeking to declare truth, and thereafter reaping the consequences, is not at the forefront of daily life. Without being the cause of discord and rarely facing true persecution from others, readiness to suffer may simply be forgotten. Perhaps we must instead ask ourselves: If asked to do so, would I be willing to suffer for Christ? Would I lay down what I value most highly, whether that be my friends, my career, my family, even my life, for the sake of following Jesus?

But remember, we're not instructed to only endure suffering, but also to rejoice in it, a concept even further outside our natural human tendencies. In Romans 5 Paul says,

"And we rejoice in the hope of the glory of God. Not only so, but we also rejoice in our sufferings, because we know that suffering produces perseverance; perseverance, character; and character, hope. And hope does not disappoint us, because God has poured out his love into our hearts by the Holy Spirit, whom he has given us."

Paul starts and ends with the promise of hope, both on an eternal scale with the glory of God and in the present through the experience of God's love. In a sermon about suffering based on this passage Pastor John Piper once said that "… the first thing we say about suffering and affliction is that God has a purpose in it. And that purpose is to bring out the patient endurance of his people for the sake of his name; and through that to test and prove and refine the reality of faith and allegiance to Christ; and through that sense of approval to strengthen and deepen and intensify our hope."

Our faithful, loving God has a purpose for us even in suffering, or perhaps *especially* in suffering. But at times we have a tendency to take matters into our own hands. We try to find ways to resolve problems on the outside, and cope with our feelings on the inside. That's where we trip and fall, easily slipping into feeling sorry for ourselves and gradually letting bitterness sneak in. God didn't tell us to try to handle it by ourselves! Instead He *"comforts us in all our troubles"* and *"poured out his love into our hearts."* He builds in us perseverance, character, and hope. Paul reminds us that:

> *"God did not give us a spirit of timidity, but a spirit of power, of love and of self-discipline. So do not be ashamed to testify about our Lord, or ashamed of me his prisoner. But join with me in suffering for the gospel, by the power of God, who has saved us and called us to a holy life— not because of anything we have done but because of his own purpose and grace"* (2nd Timothy 1:7-9).

The endurance we need is found in His power, His purpose, and His grace, not just our efforts.

For our comfort to overflow, it must be continually pouring into us.

I love that picture of our Lord pouring His love and comfort into us so that it overflows. This suggests several things. First, if we are called to comfort one another we're not in this alone. Other members of the Body of Christ are around us, sharing encouragement and love.

Second, we have to be ready to receive before trying to give. Many missionaries, pastors, psychologists, and others with similar professions burn out from constantly trying to bring comfort and healing to others, when they don't get enough themselves. The source is from above, from God, and it's only when we are full that we can effectively see that comfort overflowing into the lives of others.

Finally, I've been learning that a need for comfort is not meant to be an embarrassment, but rather a privilege, a chance to grow in faith and an opportunity to receive from God, to experience His faithfulness, and to hold on to His promise of love. We learn to declare:

"Your love, O Lord, reaches to the heavens,
your faithfulness to the skies.
Your righteousness is like the mighty
mountains, your justice like the great deep.
O Lord, you preserve both man and beast.

How priceless is your unfailing love!
Both high and low among men find refuge in
the shadow of your wings"
(Psalms 36:5-7).

Our God is Sovereign

Names used in the Bible always carry tremendous significance, both names God gives to His servants, and the names used to describe God. Many reflect His incredible power, such as "Almighty" which is used 332 times in the NIV Bible. That one seems to have a clear meaning, that God is not just mighty, but ALL Mighty, surpassing all other parts of the universe!

Another name that I've been learning a lot about is "Sovereign," which is found 293 times in the NIV translation. What's interesting about its use is that it's most common among the Major Prophets, accounting for 237 of the times used. These men declared God's sovereignty, His all-powerful rule, right next to prophesies made purely by faith in Him. Many of their prophecies were not fulfilled during their own lifespan. A large proportion of the prophecies were predicting very negative upcoming events, often received quite poorly by the authorities in power at the time. But these prophets trusted that what God says indeed happens even if they were not ones to witness it, and that His plan was flawless, despite the opposition to their pronouncements and the negative outcomes they endured.

Declaring God's sovereignty is probably most difficult when we can't understand why something is happening. Job is a good example. Scripture describes a man who followed God to the best of his ability, yet had everything he valued stripped away from his life: all material possessions, his children, even his own physical well-being.

We see the big picture of what was occurring on a supernatural level, as God declares Job's righteousness and allows Satan to attempt to challenge that. But Job didn't see that interaction. All he saw was everything he knew and loved suddenly evaporating, with no logical explanation. He didn't know that God valued him greatly enough to allow Satan's testing, or that his righteousness was being affirmed. All he was aware of was the overwhelming grief and pain surrounding him, physically, emotionally, and spiritually. The question of "Why me?" lurked in the back of his mind as he reviewed his attempts to follow

God's law and live righteously. "Did I do something to deserve this?" While he reached the point of cursing his own birthday, he stood firm in his refusal to curse God. *"Shall we accept good from God, and not trouble?"* (Job 2).

There were no easy answers, and Job lamented that *"sighing comes to me instead of food; my groans pour out like water. What I feared has come upon me; what I dreaded has happened to me. I have no peace, no quietness; I have no rest, but only turmoil"* (Job 3:24-26).

Job's three friends come to offer consolation, and at first provide needed support by just being there with him. But after one week of watching him suffer they feel the need to somehow make sense of it, to find some form of explanation for the tragedy they witnessed. What follows is a substantial portion of the book where Job's friends try to explain and rationalize his suffering, much of the time blaming Job. Eliphaz asks him, *"Is not your wickedness great? Are not your sins endless? ...If you return to the Almighty, you will be restored"* (Job 22:5, 23).

God later rebukes the three men with their claims that it's Job's fault. After all three make their arguments and Job repeatedly defends himself, a fourth man, Elihu, steps in to the picture, tired of hearing them rant with no strong argument. Elihu was younger than the others and out of respect had held his tongue, but once they had run out of explanations he could no longer resist saying what he deemed to be truth from God rather than experience from age. His main argument centers on God sovereignty and superiority to anything man could understand or justify.

> *"It is unthinkable that God would do wrong, that the Almighty would pervert justice... Out of the north he comes in golden splendor; God comes in awesome majesty. The Almighty is beyond our reach and exalted in power; in his justice and great righteousness, he does not oppress"* (Job 34:12, 37:22-23).

This monologue was one Job did not refute.

When God finally speaks to Job, He doesn't explain Himself or reveal the earlier conversation he had with Satan. Instead He declares His Sovereignty over all creation, ranging from the origin of the entire universe to the details of each animal species. *"Will the one who contends with the Almighty correct him? Let him who accuses God answer him!"* (Job 40:2). Job realizes his perspective was far too limited to question God.

Then Job replied to the LORD: "I know that you can do all things; no plan of yours can be thwarted. You asked, 'Who is this that obscures my counsel without knowledge?' Surely I spoke of things I did not understand, things too wonderful for me to know... My ears had heard of you, but now my eyes have seen you. Therefore I despise myself and repent in dust and ashes" (Job 42:1-3, 5-6).

God never told Job what had happened in supernatural realms. He taught Job to acknowledge His Sovereignty, which Job realized far surpassed anything he could imagine. Once Job recognized his need to be humbly trusting God, he was affirmed as God referred to him several times as "my servant" and rebuked the first three friends for their criticisms. God went on to not only restore Job, but to bless him more than ever before. I believe that blessing was not found solely in the prosperity given, but in the deeper knowledge of God and the ability to trust Him.

Learning to Trust

For several years, I too felt like God was teaching me to trust Him in ways I never would've grasped if living an "easy" life. Although what happened was not nearly as drastic as Job's experience, I struggled with some similar questions of God's will.

In the summer before my last year of high school I had a number of medical tests done after several people had witnessed me not responding and having trouble communicating thereafter. The tests identified the strange "episodes" I'd experienced to be complex partial seizures, abnormal brain waves from the left side of my brain that caused me to lose awareness of what was going on around me. This discovery led to MRIs that revealed a lesion in the left temporal lobe of my brain. There was no way of knowing exactly what it was, although the doctors stated that it was most likely either a hemangioma (i.e. a mass of blood vessels) or a low-grade glioma (i.e. slow-growing tumor). The initial goal was to control the seizures through medication, while keeping an eye out for any change in the lesion. At first the medication helped to some degree, but the seizures continued despite repeatedly raising the dosage.

As I left home for college I still couldn't get a driver's license and getting to know my new roommate included having to alert her that I at times had seizures. Fortunately they weren't grand mal, meaning that I didn't go into dramatic convulsions. But each time that strange feeling of déjà vu came, it was as if what was going on around me was a replaying of a videotape where I was unable to control my own words. I fought to hold on to my thoughts as they slipped away, leaving me powerless until the next thing I knew were the uncertain looks on the faces around me. My language abilities were the last to return, and there was always a frustrating window of time where I knew the meaning of what I wanted to communicate, to tell others that I was fine and it was just another seizure, but I couldn't create words to match that meaning.

Over the course of the year the seizures became worse and more frequent, even after changing to a new medication. By the time spring break arrived, brain surgery became a real possibility, there being few treatment options for "intractable" epilepsy.

Some diseases have perpetual symptoms, such as pain or tiredness, but a person may learn how to compensate for such challenges. The problem with seizures is that you never know when they will sneak up on you. Any decision I made about going somewhere or doing something had an extra question tacked on: *What if I have a seizure?* If I were getting to know someone, when would it be appropriate to tell them the reality I faced? When starting each semester I had to alert my new professors so that they would not "freak out" if I wasn't responding in class (which did occur).

There are few ways to feel more helpless or vulnerable than losing the capacity to control one's own mind. Each time it occurred around others I felt humiliated and did everything I could to downplay the event. I didn't want this struggle to be a center point of my identity. In my pride I asked my parents to keep mention of it minimal in family updates; as one of five siblings I didn't want to be identified as "the one who has seizures."

Like Job, I struggled with God's reasoning to allow this to happen, looking for some justification or explanation. It was one thing to suffer for Christ, where there appeared to be value in standing firm for one's faith. But these unpredictable, unexplainable physical trials seemed to have no purpose whatsoever.

Epilepsy was something I wanted to hide, what I felt as almost degrading. But it forced me to learn several things, particularly vulnerability. There were times when I had to swallow my pride and ask for help, both from God and from others around me, whether getting a ride to somewhere I needed to go or receiving a comforting hug. I was a good student, but intelligence didn't help one bit when facing seizures, and after missing a class I had to ask for notes and accept that not every grade had to be an A. As I approached summer and the prospect of surgery, I also had to be open on a larger scale, so as to ask for prayer from friends and supporters of our family. And in the midst of uncertainty I had to learn to trust God.

Several events took place at the end of the semester, before returning from Washington to California. The day before leaving the college, a friend and I decided to attempt what we'd been scheming about for some time—to climb a huge tree that had a rope hanging down and near the top, barely visible from the ground, swung a hammock.

The tree viewed from across the pond.

With uncertainty about the results of the surgery and whether I'd be back the next semester, I felt it could be my last chance to make such an attempt. The first branches were 20 to 25 feet off the ground, and with the rope dangling just above our heads, we ended up borrowing a ladder from the art department to give us a boost. My body was not in optimal condition, and the first time I tried I felt shaky and let my friend go instead. When she came down, I decided to give it one last attempt. I managed to hoist myself up the rope to the first two branches, but with one shaky arm over each one and no foothold I was paralyzed. Suddenly I felt myself falling, followed by a moment of intense pain as I hit the ground while simultaneously going into a seizure.

As I came out of the seizure I heard the ambulance approaching, but in warbled speech tried to explain that I wasn't unconscious, I had just had a seizure, and despite their admonishments I got myself to my feet. Once able to communicate I adamantly refused to go with the paramedics to the ER. "You just fell 25 feet. You might be in shock." "I'm fine. And I don't have time. I have to pack and leave tomorrow." My whole body was in pain for days, but when walking away with no broken bones I realized I must have had God's protection, perhaps some "angelic cushioning" for the impact. *Maybe He's keeping me alive for a reason.*

I spent the next two weeks at a Christian service project nearby, and during that time encountered waves of emotions. I realized that I was afraid of being afraid, worried that when I faced surgery I'd be unable to cope. But that didn't happen. God again showed His protection on the drive with a friend through rainy mountain roads, heading toward Seattle to catch a flight. A windshield wiper suddenly lost a screw, and although we were able to remove the blade, the remaining metal piece eventually appeared to start leaving a scratch mark. Most of the narrow road had no shoulder, and seeing a short patch of gravel ahead led to a quick decision to pull over, but with a rapid brake the velocity carried us too far. For a second the tilting van appeared to consider rolling into the ditch below, but it instead settled, and shortly thereafter a police car drove by and the officer kindly called a tow truck.

After the escapade, I flew down to California, still processing all that had occurred and the fact that I was still alive. In preparation for surgery I had a whole array of tests, both mental and physical, but did not find myself overly anxious. When talking to one of the doctors who conducted a test battery, she questioned me as to how I was dealing with all that was going on. I told her that I had a God who had proven Himself faithful and was continuing to do so. I wrote an e-mail to my supporters:

> I was reading in Habakkuk, and was blessed by the words that no matter what the circumstances "I will rejoice in the LORD, I will be joyful in God my Savior. The Sovereign LORD is my strength; he makes my feet like the feet of a deer, he enables me to go on the heights." (Habakkuk 3:18-19). Two or three weeks from now it looks pretty certain that I'll be getting a part of my brain removed, yet somehow I feel neither discouraged nor afraid. By His grace God has brought me this far up the rocky terrain, and I know He can take me the rest of the way.

When going into surgery, things were completely out of my control. There was a possibility I could die if something went wrong, I could lose mental capacity to some degree, or I could receive bad news about what was in my brain. I had to trust both the hands of the surgeon, and on a broader scale trust the perfect plans of God. I could in no way look to my own knowledge, skills, or intelligence; they had absolutely no bearing on the process or outcome. Instead, I could say, *"Praise be to the Lord, to God our Savior, who daily bears our burdens. Our God is a God who saves; from the Sovereign Lord comes escape from death"* (Psalm 68:19-20). This verse captures both releasing our simple daily concerns and trusting Him with our lives. I was at a place where the two coincided, and had to declare that He was Sovereign over my life.

God did preserve my life, but the struggle wasn't over. I managed to get out of the hospital in three days, still able to move, think, speak, and very grateful to be home. A couple of weeks later I got the news that the test showed the lesion to be an astrocytoma, a type of tumor that has a higher tendency than others to grow back, usually at a higher grade. There was some residual tissue still there, meaning an increased risk for recurrence or progression. And a couple weeks after that, I had another seizure. I was devastated. At that time I journaled:

Why? Why isn't it over yet? Why do more factors keep coming into the picture? Why can't I have closure? Why can't I just keep going on with life and not constantly deal with this? Why the perpetual process of disappointments and falling back to where I was before, only now with less hope for what's next? Why can't I just spend my time reaching out to others and working to prepare myself academically for the rest of my life and ministry? Why does dealing with seizures, doctors, tests, and other medical aspects continue? Will it continue? How many more options do I have? Will it get worse? How are you using this for your glory, Lord? What's next? Should I hope for the best, and again have chance for an overwhelming disappointment?

In the Hands of the Potter

Somehow, I hadn't yet learned to fully trust God. Like Job, I questioned my circumstances, searching for some explanation, or at least for some form of meaning. I think most of us have that tendency to want answers. We quickly ask "why" as if we expect or believe we deserve a rationalization for the difficulties endured.

When something doesn't go the way we want, and we can't see what's coming around the corner, we forget that there is a much bigger picture, one that actually spreads across time and space, not contained by our own limited understanding. We live in temporary, mortal bodies and in this state, in this broken world, we will face challenges. That's a given. But when considering the eternal picture those challenges should be trumped by God's Sovereignty and His decision and ability to use us, even in our obviously imperfect state.

"But we have this treasure in jars of clay to show that this all-surpassing power is from God and not from us. We are hard pressed on every side, but not crushed; perplexed, but not in despair; persecuted, but not abandoned; struck down, but not destroyed. We always carry around in our body the death of Jesus, so that the life of Jesus may also be revealed in our body. For we who are alive are always being given over to death for Jesus' sake, so that his life may be revealed in our mortal body."
(2 Corinthians 4:7-11)

Clay jars are temporary, and even if well-crafted they cannot remain permanently in perfect condition, gradually eroding or easily broken. Their utility and value usually come from what is put inside them. I think our current culture emphasizes the importance of making your own pot look good. Perhaps we should decorate our jars, make them look efficient, let people know how useful they are. We place a lot of value on physical attributes. It does not take too many TV commercials to illustrate the value placed on appearance, whether covering it with make-up or trying to change it with the latest weight-loss diet.

Visible accomplishments are constantly applauded, with hundreds of self-help books telling us how to succeed, how to "sell" ourselves. But isn't the perpetual focus on how others perceive us a distraction from the worth of what is inside? The Maker has offered true Life to fill our jars. There are many claims about the right thing to put in your jar. Maybe it's satisfaction; we see all the ads for how to make yourself feel better. Maybe it's a search for meaning by doing good deeds; that is emphasized in many religions. But God, the Creator, offers us the treasure of His glory, the power of His Spirit, and the life that comes from His loving grace. That far surpasses anything the world offers, and it is the only option that will last for eternity.

Clay jars can't do anything by themselves. It is the owner who decides how to use them, when to use them, where to put them. Rather than putting the focus on ourselves and pronouncing the best way for us to be used or displayed, our job is to carry the eternal life given us, and to let God use us to take it to others around us. And there is not a limited amount of life to hold or distribute. It is once again the picture of overflowing. We are vessels of God's love, and are constantly being offered refills.

But we have to be ready to trust His plan for where He wants us regardless of our understanding of the current circumstances. It is when we focus on ourselves that we get distracted. Rather than question my own ability to serve God, I must remember that He has an all-surpassing power to use me. On the other side of that, rather than inform God where and how I would be most useful, I must relinquish my plans and expectations.

In the same way each of us must continue surrendering ownership to Him, and seeing it as a privilege to be included in His perfect plan. Yes, we'll face times when we're hard-pressed and perplexed, unable to grasp the reason or the ultimate outcome for our circumstances. But we are not crushed, not abandoned, not destroyed. Instead the Potter is right next to us the entire time.

Later in the same passage Paul concludes:

"Therefore we do not lose heart. Though outwardly we are wasting away, yet inwardly we are being renewed day by day. For our light and momentary troubles are achieving for us an eternal glory that far outweighs them all. So we fix our eyes not on what is seen, but on what is unseen. For

what is seen is temporary, but what is unseen is eternal" (vs. 16-18).

It's easy for us to get wrapped up in the temporary, whether health problems, or finances, or decisions, or any other everyday source of stress. Focusing on those issues will leave us frustrated and depressed. There are always unanswered questions, many of which will probably remain unanswered as long as we are on this earth. Job had the same misgivings: *"Your hands shaped me and made me. Will you now turn and destroy me? Remember that you molded me like clay. Will you now turn me to dust again?" (Job 10:8-9).* Job was able to recognize God's power over his life, but could not understand His motive for allowing hardship. He perceived the Creator as becoming a destroyer, but although he was struck down, he was not destroyed. From his limited perspective he was unable to know that God was indeed crediting his righteousness.

God has a much bigger perspective, one that crosses all barriers of time and space. He didn't explain Himself to Job, He simply showed Job His Sovereignty. Isaiah also warns us, *"Woe to him who quarrels with his Maker... Does the clay say to the potter, 'What are you making?' Does your work say, 'He has no*

The Master Potter creates each of us as a unique vessel,
and can care for it and use it when we allow him to do so.

hands'?" (Isaiah 45:9). It seems rather silly to be trying to tell God the right way to make us or use us. Instead we should ask Him: What are You trying to teach me through this situation? How would you like to use me even in these painful circumstances? How can I be a vessel of Your light and love today?

I praise God that He puts up with our questions, just as He did with Job. Having made us, He knows exactly what we need and where our weak points are, and can keep us from being crushed. He also has given us strengths and can use us for greater purposes than we could ever imagine. We have the promise that He loves us, His creation, constantly, and has offered us an eternal glory that far surpasses anything we face in the temporary, mortal state.

Our God is Glorious

For a long time before facing physical problems I may have been able to say that the purpose of life is to glorify God, the "correct," Sunday School answer. But life experiences put the concept of glorifying God in a different light, somehow allowing it to become more real and carry a deeper meaning.

I may have previously equated bringing glory to God with seeing advances in His kingdom, watching others come to Christ, planting a church in an unreached people group, or other aspects of "helping" Him look bigger and better from the human perspective. That may be a subtle reflection of what we perceive as glorification (even if we don't use that word) for people— essentially an increase in fame and power. But when taking a step back and looking at it in a different light I don't think His glory rests on what we see as accomplishments. The psalmist wrote:

"Teach me your way, O LORD, and I will walk in your truth; give me an undivided heart that I may fear your name. I will praise you, O Lord my God, with all my heart; I will glorify your name forever" (Psalm 86:11-12).

"My soul will boast in the LORD; let the afflicted hear and rejoice. Glorify the LORD with me; let us exalt his name together" (Psalm 34: 2-3).

Both of these verses come as a response to God working in us, not us working for Him. Giving glory to Him comes out of joy. We are certainly called to "declare His glory among the nations" (Psalm 96:3), but we cannot control their response. With our limited power we can't take it as our responsibility to "make sure" they glorify Him. We are not alone in declaring God's majesty; His creation, the heavens and the earth, get to do the same thing.

God's infinite glory is already in place; it has been there for eternity, and nothing we do will make it bigger or brighter. It is His very nature, His essence of perfection and holiness, and thus far surpasses our ability to understand or even see it to its fullest. When Moses met God on Mt. Sinai, God told him he was pleased with him. Moses had one response: "Now, show me your glory." But God told Moses that "no one may see me and live." He allowed Moses to glimpse just the back of Him, but not His face. Just that much left Moses with a face so radiant that the other Israelites couldn't handle it, and he had to wear a veil (Exodus 33-34). Why? Because as sinful people we humans are cut off from God's holiness and therefore His glory.

The sinful chasm between us and God can only be crossed by Christ's redemption. Perhaps seeing what happened in the Old Testament, such as the encounter Moses had, shows the significance of the glory cited in the New Testament. John makes the statement in the first chapter of his gospel: *"The Word became flesh and made his dwelling place among us. We have seen his glory, the glory of the One and Only, who came from the Father, full of grace and truth."*

The angels' announcement of the birth of Jesus ended with the climactic declaration: *"Glory to God in the highest, and on earth peace to men on whom his favor rests."* Was this because of the accomplishments of a newborn infant? Or was it a celebration of God's glory drawing closer to a fallen world? Paul clearly stated that *"all have sinned and fallen short of the glory of God,"* but follows that with the good news that we are *"justified freely by his grace through the redemption that came by Christ Jesus"* (Romans 3:23-24).

Just before His trial, Jesus had His prayer time with the Father, asking for glory. *"I have brought you glory on earth by completing the work you gave me to do. And now, Father, glorify me in your presence with the glory I had with you before the world began"* (John 17:3-4). Jesus declared that He had brought God glory, and immediately after was beaten, scorned, abandoned, and crucified. He hadn't established an expansive kingdom; He hadn't reached the ends of the earth; in fact, He had very few followers who remained faithful. The Jewish expectation for a powerful Messiah who would overcome the Roman Empire and establish his reign was not met. By human standards Jesus was dishonored, not glorified. But He had made it possible for us to experience God's glory through redemptive grace. That was His primary purpose for coming to earth.

Somehow, encountering the previously frightening holiness of God's glory became a promise, a reward. Unlike Moses, we are invited to not only see, but to take part in His glory. Paul mentions it several times in his letters as an encouragement: *"Set your mind on things above, not on earthly things. For you died, and your life is now hidden with Christ in God. When Christ, who is your life, appears, then you also will appear with him in glory"* (Colossians 3:2-4). This verse holds being with Christ in both present and future tense. It may be our tendency to assume the promise of glory is limited to the eternal joys of heaven, in part because of the difficulty in perceiving or even imagining the glory of God, particularly after reading accounts like that of Moses. But Paul says that we are NOW hidden with Christ in God. Yes, there is certainly more to come that is beyond our current comprehension, but it starts in our lives once we take on our new identity in Christ.

We have to look at things from an entirely different perspective when living for God's glory, because it's no longer something out in the distance, but can be manifested within us. For *"we, who with unveiled faces all reflect the Lord's glory, are being transformed into his likeness with ever-increasing glory, which comes from the Lord, who is the Spirit"* (2 Corinthians 3:14). God is NOW transforming us to become more like Him, including His glorious nature. It is not based on our abilities, but rather our release of the old, sinful self and allowing God to fill that void with His love.

The shift in perspective means looking at life on an eternal scale rather than a temporary, earthly scale. Jesus wasn't upset that He no longer had tens of thousands following Him; He saw what glory His life would bring for eternity, including through our reflections of Him. Our standards of accomplishment simply do not apply. It's not how much money we donate, how many people we tell about Christ, how high a level of leadership we hold, how many results we can see from the efforts we made, or how much praise we receive from those around us.

Rather, it is how much we are living out the glory of Christ in thought, word, and action, even when seen by no one other than God. In times of feeling weak, unproductive, lacking in influence, or simply not being recognized for effort, it is comforting to know that glory is not something to be achieved by our own merit. The human form of glorification becomes irrelevant when our desire is to die to the sinful, human self. Instead we live to put the focus back on God, and the way He is at work in and through us.

Surrendering All

For the sake of God's glory, Jesus set an example for us by completely surrendering His life. He told His disciples, *"The reason my Father loves me is that I lay down my life— only to take it up again. No one takes it from me, but I lay it down of my own accord. I have authority to lay it down and authority to take it up again. This command I received from my Father"* (John 10:17-18). He does not lay down His life out of defeat, but instead states His very power over death.

This paradox of submission and supremacy coincides with the temporal, earthly events and the eternal significance. Submitting to death, and in it displaying His humanity, was necessary to show authority over death. In order for the resurrection to take place the burial had to first occur. Yet it required voluntary suffering, not only physically, but in bearing the sin of the world, the essence of death.

This action of atonement provided us with a means of access to God in His holiness, but free will remains. It becomes our responsibility to choose between life and death. When we choose Him He calls us to follow His example, to surrender every aspect of our lives at the foot of the cross. A similar paradox forms: dying to self in order to find true life in Christ.

We give up our citizenship in this world not to live empty lives, but because, as Paul said, *"our citizenship is in heaven. And we eagerly await a Savior from there, the Lord Jesus Christ, who by the power that enables him to bring everything under his control, will transform our lowly bodies so that they will be like his glorious body"* (Philippians 3:20-21). These verses confirm the eternal hope we have. Regardless of whether or not we choose to follow Christ, we know our time on this earth, in these physical bodies, will not last forever. It seems our earthly desires so easily become higher priority, despite the relatively short (on an eternal scale) amount of time we have here. We often need to reevaluate what is of greatest importance and how much we are willing to give up.

I love the song written in 1896 by Judson W. Van DeVenter:

All to Jesus, I surrender;
All to Him I freely give;
I will ever love and trust Him,
In His presence daily live.

I surrender all, I surrender all.
All to Thee, my blessèd Savior,
I surrender all.

All to Jesus I surrender;
Humbly at His feet I bow,
Worldly pleasures all forsaken;
Take me, Jesus, take me now.

All to Jesus, I surrender;
Make me, Savior, wholly Thine;
Let me feel the Holy Spirit,
Truly know that Thou art mine.

All to Jesus, I surrender;
Lord, I give myself to Thee;
Fill me with Thy love and power;
Let Thy blessing fall on me.

All to Jesus I surrender;
Now I feel the sacred flame.
O the joy of full salvation!
Glory, glory, to His Name!

The song traces the process of giving up what's important to us, an easy, comfortable life, to accepting what is far greater in value: eternal salvation and the privilege of taking part in God's glory. What was hardest for me to surrender was my capacity to be independent and productive, my ability to make a difference in the lives of others, and my desire to be thought well of by others.

After discovering that brain surgery had not fully solved the problem, I ended up having what is termed "gamma knife radiation" six months later during my winter break. It was done in one session, with my head pinned into a frame and the radiation being on a single area. During the following months I had a glimmer of hope that the struggle was over when having no seizures.

Soon after the semester ended, the constant exhaustion and intense headaches I felt led to another MRI that looked simply horrible. The first assumption was that it was a delayed reaction to the radiation, and I was immediately given medication to bring down the inflammation. But a few days later the results of a PET scan came in: *It's a re-growth of the tumor; you'll need an emergency surgery.* I had done plenty of research, and knew that for a brain tumor to grow that big, that quickly meant it was probably malignant, and such patients tend to live less than a year. All my summer plans were cancelled as I went to the hospital a couple of days later. Because of the neurosurgeon's full schedule, after hours of waiting I was told to come back the next day. When I arrived I found out that the latest MRI showed a decrease in size of the inflamed area. The logical conclusion was that the medication helped reduce the inflammation, suggesting it was in fact a reaction instead of a regrowth. This was a relief, but the saga was not yet over.

With plans cancelled, I ended up staying with my parents most of the summer. The medication quickly started to produce side effects: my hands got shaky and I couldn't sleep well. My immune system also went downhill, leading to the development of a nasty abscess. Each time we tried to reduce the dosage of the medication, the headache crept back in as the inflammation increased.

I didn't want to give up my plans to spend the fall semester volunteering in Thailand, and determined to go despite my doctor's reservations. But my body continued to deteriorate as I remained on the medication that increased the levels of cortisol in my system. In the midst of adjusting to a new climate, a new setting, a new culture, I also struggled with the physical changes occurring. My hair was falling out, my faulty immune

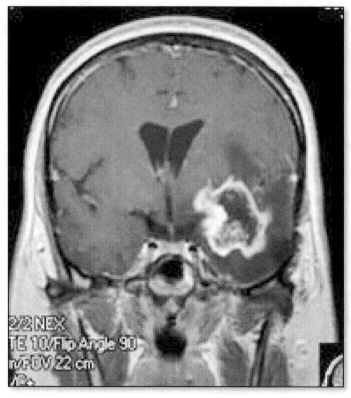

Nine months after the reaction occurred the inflammation and edema were still evident.

system left me with a cold for almost a month, I gained weight, stretch marks started appearing on my thinned skin, and I soon had a rounded "moon face," among other side effects. Even more troubling were my mental capacities: I couldn't think quite as clearly and was often forgetting things. It was as if someone had pushed fast forward on my body clock and I was suddenly an old woman. By the time I went for some time in a different city in Thailand, I was practically unrecognizable. Yet I did not want to simply give up and leave, which I saw as defeat.

His Strength in My Weakness

During this time of physical weaknesses I struggled with questions of why God was allowing them. Was I not trying to serve Him? Many people had prayed for my health, some implying that if I just had enough faith I'd be miraculously healed. One time I was at a missions conference in Latin America, and part way through the week a few of the people there found out about my physical struggles and asked that the whole group pray for me, declaring they were sure healing would come. I could not perceive any changes the next day, and felt awkward when attempting to respond to those who expectantly asked me how I was.

I had never heard God specifically promise healing for my body. Instead, I identified more like Paul, who also had a challenging, probably physical condition, his "thorn in the flesh." Three times he asked God (with more than enough faith) to take it away.

"But [the Lord] said to me, 'My grace is sufficient for you, for my power is made perfect in weakness.' Therefore I will boast all the more gladly about my weaknesses, so that Christ's power may rest on me. That is why, for Christ's sake, I delight in weaknesses, in insults, in hardships, in persecutions, in difficulties. For when I am weak, then I am strong" (2 Corinthians 12:9-10).

I did not want to admit my weakness. For a while I was constantly trying to convince myself that I could go on, and more than anything dreaded feeling like I was a burden to others. I did end up leaving Thailand earlier than I had originally planned, and after visiting my family in Uzbekistan I returned to the US. There I repeatedly saw close friends who didn't recognize me and upon returning to school found myself struggling to simply keep up on reading assignments, a challenge I had never experienced. In many facets of life I felt weak. I had to learn a lot more about humility and about dependence on God instead of myself. I had to surrender both my present situation and possible future outcomes to Him.

It was during that time of weakness, particularly while in Thailand, that I experienced God closer than ever before. I turned to Him for strength on a regular basis, and He responded. At the time I was waking up in the middle of the night almost every night, and one of those times, I felt God prodding me to get up and go to the window. I finally did, and looked out over the trees as a few clouds floated across the dark sky.

At that moment I had the thought in my mind: *Wouldn't it be amazing to see a shooting star?* Seconds later, just as I was telling myself not to be silly, a shooting star flashed by right where I was looking. It seemed as if God was chuckling, reminding me of His power over all creation. That night was just one of the numerous times I felt I had a dialogue with God, not just a monologue of my own requests and complaints. He pointed out areas that I was holding on to lies, and replaced those with His loving truths.

During this life chapter of physical and emotional trials God gave me a promise from 1st Peter:

Looking out over the trees I was amazed to see a
shooting star right after the thought came to mind.

"In this you greatly rejoice, though now for a little while you may have had to suffer grief in all kinds of trials. These have come so that your faith—of greater worth than gold, which perishes even though refined by fire— may be proved genuine and may result in praise, glory and honor when Jesus Christ is revealed" (I Peter 1: 6-8).

For gold to be refined it must be put in the heat until liquefied, at which point the impurities are removed from the top, having separated from the pure gold. The crude metal is not just tossed in the fire and abandoned, but must be carefully monitored as the layers of scum separate and are removed by the Refiner. This process has to occur before the precious metal can be shaped into something of value, something considered beautiful. Our faith also starts in a crude state, with pieces of our own warped beliefs and perceptions conglomerating with God's truth. What comes from us must be separated from what comes from God, and for that refining to take place, heat is necessary, even though painful.

If nothing else, I believe God used those times of weakness to refine my faith, and allow me to draw closer to His glory. He knows the pain that comes when going through the fire, and even weeps with us when we cry out to Him. Those are the times when He helps remove some of the impurities that hinder our growth in faith. God also knows how to bring us closer to Himself. I hear the saying that "God won't give someone more than they can handle," but I truly believe that there are times when God allows us to encounter what is beyond our own limited capacities to manage alone. But there is absolutely nothing that is too big for us to stand against through dependence on His power.

One of the key steps to partaking in God's glory is putting our own temporary glories aside. For me, it's still hard to "boast" about my weaknesses like Paul did, but I continue to ask God to show His power in and around me. Moses had his weaknesses, so much so that he needed his brother to be able to talk to Pharaoh, but he was still called by God and given the privilege of being in His glorious presence.

God doesn't expect us to be perfect and glorious before we start to follow Him and serve Him; instead He takes us with our blemishes and uses us in ways we never would have come close to matching by our own strength. So I ask of Him now: *"Not to us, O Lord, not to us but to your name be the glory, because of your love and faithfulness"* (Psalm 115:1). Use me, even in my weakness, to bring glory to your name, whether as a vessel of your love to others or even just here in my own heart.

"To him who is able to keep you from falling and to present you before his glorious presence without fault and with great joy— to the only God our Savior be glory and majesty, power and authority, through Jesus Christ our Lord, before all ages, now and forever more. Amen" (Jude 24).

Our God is Gracious

After thinking about God's incredible glory, I find it more and more amazing that He invites us to take part in that. The Presence of God was very significant throughout the Old Testament, as He guided His people out of Egypt and through the desert in a cloud by day and fire by night. It was because of His Presence that the Israelites received their daily nourishment in the desert and won their victories in the Promised Land. For the more intimate aspect of His Presence, God commanded them to dedicate a space for Him, first in the tabernacle, eventually in the temple. Because of sin, humans were separated from His Holy Presence. Only the priest went into the Most Holy of Holies, a significant event that occurred once a year after purification rituals and offerings of atonement to cover any sin or impurities. By Mosaic Law only the righteous could enter God's true presence, and sins had to be paid for by sacrifices.

Jesus came with the new covenant of grace. Paul wrote, *"This righteousness from God comes through faith in Jesus Christ to all who believe. There is no difference, for all have sinned and fall short of the glory of God, and are justified freely by his grace through the redemption that came by Christ Jesus"* (Romans 3:22-23). The need for righteousness to enter God's holy presence remained, but Jesus paid the ultimate price for our sins. Salvation and justification were not granted out of obligation, but as a true gift of love.

"In love he predestined us to be adopted as his sons through Jesus Christ, in accordance with his pleasure and will—to the praise of his glorious grace, which he has freely given us in the One he loves. In him we have redemption through his blood, the forgiveness of sins, in accordance with the riches of God's grace that he lavished on us with all wisdom and understanding" (Ephesians 1:4-8).

We never earned God's grace. He knew us as His children before time began, and wanted that joy for us. That's why He sent Jesus. *"From the fullness of his grace we have all received one blessing after another. For the law was given through Moses; grace and truth came through Jesus Christ"* (John 1:16-17). God didn't give grace just to get us past the minimum criteria so we could sneak into heaven. He gave it as a blessing of freedom to be in His presence our entire lives, even while on this sinful earth. When we recognize His glory, and surrender every part of our lives, we empty ourselves so that He can fill us instead with His grace.

We sometimes trivialize the act of coming into God's presence. Going to church on Sundays shouldn't be just another event on the calendar, something done by obligation. It's an opportunity to join others in together entering His Presence! God's grace allows us all to be a part of the "royal priesthood," to not only witness from afar but to partake in His glory this very day. No longer do we depend on one priest to act as the go-between, nor is God's presence (as we perceive it) limited to a single building. Instead we are called "temples," dwelling places for God. And this isn't limited to Sunday mornings. The chasm of sin that separated us from God is crossed by Christ's sacrifice.

"But because of his great love for us, God, who is rich in mercy, made us alive with

Christ even when we were dead in transgressions—it is by grace you have been saved. And God raised us up with Christ and seated us with him in the heavenly realms in Christ Jesus, in order that in the coming ages he might show the incomparable riches of his grace, expressed in his kindness to us in Christ Jesus. For it is by grace you have been saved, through faith—and this not from yourselves, it is the gift of God—not by works, so that no one can boast" (Ephesians 2:4-9).

These verses of promise include the eternal hope of being raised up, just as Christ was not conquered by the grave, but overcame death forever. That victory extends to us through His grace, for there is no way for us to earn our salvation for eternity. And it is not only a distant promise for the next life; the salvation has already come and we are already made spiritually alive.

Being alive with Christ means being filled with the Holy Spirit, so that we are perpetually in His Presence. *"He saved us through the washing of rebirth and renewal by the Holy Spirit, whom he poured out on us generously through Jesus Christ our Savior, so that, having been justified by his grace, we might become heirs having the hope of eternal life"* (Titus 3:5-7). We are given this picture of cleansing, beginning a new life no longer governed by guilt. Despite our ongoing faults and failures, by grace we are forgiven and renewed.

Each day should be lived to the fullest, knowing that the Source of Life resides in us and allowing Him to do the leading. If the Israelites could follow God when in the cloud above them, can't we follow His guidance from within our lives? We love the tangible and visible, and when compared to the clear evidence of guidance that Israel had in the desert, seeking direction may now seem more ambiguous. But it is here that the opportunity to grow in faith is present, as we trust in the unseen. As we continue to hand control back to God, our faith grows, pushing us closer to Him and allowing us to become more aware of His presence. As a result, our thoughts, words, and actions can better reflect His love and grace.

When Paul dealt with his weakness, God told him, "My grace is sufficient." From then on Paul rejoiced in his weakness because he accepted his need for grace, the same grace that allows us to enter the Presence of our Holy God.

One of the areas I struggled with throughout my times of weakness was feeling like I was a failure and a burden to others. Coming from an impressive family, I easily compared myself to my older sisters. *If they are so successful in every area of life, why did I end up like this?* While my family was continually loving and supportive, I at times felt guilty accepting anything when I felt I couldn't give much in return. Many times I had to rely on help from others, getting rides during my years without a driver's license, receiving care when recovering from surgery, even the needed hugs and words of encouragement.

Just as it may be difficult to receive from other people when unable to reciprocate, it seems we do the same with the grace offered from God. We easily fall into "works," trying to earn what was given freely. I think one of the things God was trying to teach me was to accept love, both from Him and from others.

During my last week in Thailand I'd been reading a book on prayer that mentioned the significance of names, referencing the many times throughout the Bible that God gave or changed an individual's name, providing a specific meanings. After Jacob had a night wrestling with God he was called Israel, or "he struggled with God." Samuel name meant "heard of God," and he became a prominent priest and prophet. Jesus' disciple Simon was re-named Peter, "the Rock," becoming a cornerstone in the early church. The book suggested spending time asking God what name He would give you.

As I sat under the stars and prayed, the words came to my mind, *"What is your middle name?"* Grace. At first I brushed it off, but that same passage came to mind. *My grace is sufficient for you.* A bit later I had a brief phone conversation with my mom, who, with no knowledge of my interaction with God, closed by telling me to remember my middle name. Grace. Another friend had e-mailed me from the US, also mentioning that passage. At that point I wasn't completely sure what to make of it, but saw it as closely connected to handing my weaknesses back to God in exchange for His grace.

Grace is not earned, it is only accepted as a gift. And it isn't doled out in small helpings, but given in abundance. *"For if, by the trespass of the one man, death reigned through that one man, how much more will those who receive God's abundant provision of grace and of the gift of righteousness reign in life through the one man, Jesus Christ"* (Romans 5:17). In this verse the promise of reigning in life comes with only one qualification: that we receive an abundant gift of grace. It seems an offer that is hard to turn down, yet even today so many of us continue to try to earn life, getting wrapped up in legalism, guilt, or comparing ourselves to each other. Our weaknesses can be seen as an effective reminder of our limitations and need for grace rather than demeaning evidence of our lack of value. We simply have to put aside our pride to receive the extravagant gift being offered.

A Reason to Rejoice

So how should we respond to this incredible gift of grace? I think this is where our call to rejoice comes in. I earlier mentioned Paul's encouraging words in Romans 5:1-5:

"Therefore..., we have peace with God through our Lord Jesus Christ, through whom we have gained access by faith into this grace in which we now stand. And we rejoice in the hope of the glory of God. Not only so, but we also rejoice in our sufferings, because we know that suffering produces perseverance; perseverance, character; and character, hope. And hope does not disappoint us, because God has poured out his love into our hearts by the Holy Spirit, whom he has given us."

Notice that Paul not only includes suffering, but emphasizes it as what builds up our perseverance, character, and finally hope. Hope is what brings us to a spirit of rejoicing, depending not on what we know or are currently experiencing, but rather the promise God gave us. Hope in God's love remains as constant as God's Presence, regardless of circumstances that we may be facing.

I don't think rejoicing is the same as the modern concept of being happy. We might not be happy about a particularly difficult set of circumstances, but can still rejoice! Joy is listed as the second fruit of the Spirit, right between love and peace. It is a result of what may come from letting the Holy Spirit infiltrate every part of who we are. As we continue to grow spiritually, we can learn to rejoice at a deeper, more sincere level.

When we enter the Presence of God because of His grace we have reason to rejoice. As we begin to look at our lives from an eternal perspective, the suffering itself is reason to rejoice, just as Peter wrote, *"But rejoice that you participate in the sufferings of Christ, so that you may be overjoyed when his glory is revealed"* (1 Peter 4:13). Christ suffered for our salvation, and if we reflect on how He suffered not only physically, but in bearing the weight of the sin of all humanity, it puts our trivial challenges in perspective. He understands our pain, but also sets an example for us, reminding us of the eternal ramifications for current sufferings, and offering us a chance to grow closer to Him.

Oh, how encouraging that suffering can be a way to identify with Christ, a chance to draw nearer to Him! While our team in Kazakhstan expected to be on trial the day we remembered Jesus being on trial, our tiny taste of pain was put into a new perspective. When I was questioning how much longer I had to live because of a brain tumor, what source of hope I had for knowing that to live was Christ, to die was gain. As I struggled with utter weakness, what comfort it was to know that God could use even that to show His grace and power. And when I felt judged by others for not having "enough faith" to be healed, the value of suffering as a reason to rejoice put the circumstances in a different light.

Yet, it is often very challenging to focus on rejoicing in the middle of each difficult circumstance. I cannot say that I went through these experiences always wearing a smile, nor are we expected to do so. Even Jesus felt grief and anger in various situations. But emotions can be differentiated from attitude, the former being our natural, human reactions and the latter relying on our choice in how to respond to those reactions.

It can take great effort to find joy, such that Paul emphatically tells the recipients of his letters: *"Rejoice in the Lord always. I will say it again: Rejoice!"* (Philippians 4:4) and *"Be joyful always; pray continually, give thanks in all circumstances, for this is God's will for you in Christ Jesus"* (1 Thessalonians 5:16-18). The Ability to be constantly joyful may seem outside our capacities, but we are not called to do by our own strength. These commands are written to churches or communities of believers, not individuals, just as we are called to build each other up. And sandwiched between joy and giving thanks is "pray continually," as we return to God and receive His love and grace. This choice to draw near to Him allows for the transformation into His likeness that reshapes our perception of circumstances.

Drawing closer to God does not mean we immediately manage to start living up to His standards of holiness. It may not even equate to making an effort to think, act, and speak in a way that follows His commands, at least not when depending on our own capacities. I'd say that new patterns of thoughts and actions are the by-products of allowing Him to fill us with His grace. Instead of it being us living for Him, I believe it's more allowing Him to live through us. This does not mean taking a passive stance;

indeed it requires effort and discipline to draw near and surrender our lives to God on a regular basis. We so easily slip back into self-centered patterns, often calling for repentance to turn back to Him. Yet He always welcomes us back, and rejoices each time. So also should we rejoice that despite our faults His loving arms remain open.

God is the ultimate source of life, and as we allow Him to fill us daily with His holy Presence, we are able to better reflect His glory. That's when the fruit of the Spirit described in Galatians 5:22 come forth in love, joy, peace, patience, kindness, goodness, faithfulness, gentleness, and self-control. As our relationship with Christ deepens, we begin to allow Him into the dark corners of hearts, and His Presence replaces sin and sorrow with His joy, the joy that comes from glorifying Him and living in His love.

How lovely is your dwelling place, O LORD Almighty! My soul yearns, even faints for the courts of the LORD; my heart and my flesh cry out for the living God... Blessed are those who dwell in your house; they are ever praising you (Psalm 84: 1-2, 4).

Sharing the Gift of Abundant Love

Jesus served as the perfect example of living out the Presence of God through His *agape,* His unconditional love. Following that loving example brings joy:

"As the Father has loved me, so have I loved you. Now remain in my love. If you obey my commands, you will remain in my love, just as I have obeyed my Father's commands and remain in his love. I have told you this so that my joy may be in you and that your joy may be complete. My command is this: Love each other as I have loved you. Greater love has no one than this, that he lay down his life for his friends" (John 15:9-13).

It seems that a lot of our reason to rejoice comes from both receiving and giving love. The nature of God's love could be explored for thousands of pages without being fully understood, but for now we will only briefly reflect on what it means in the "love each other" context. We do not participate in the glory of Christ solely as individuals. Instead we are called to be a part of the Body of Christ.

We're not expected to each be a self-sufficient representation of Christ. Rather, we join together with other believers, all filled by the same Spirit. Being part of a larger entity does not mean losing our individual identities. Within that body we still are unique, with gifts and skills we can share with the rest of the Body of believers.

"The human body has many parts, but the many parts make up only one body. So it is with the body of Christ... we have all been baptized into Christ's body by one Spirit, and we have all received the same Spirit... God made our bodies with many parts, and he has put each part just where he wants it. What a strange thing a body would be if it had only one part! Yes, there are many parts, but only one body.
So God has put the body together in such a way that extra honor and care are given to those parts that have less dignity. This makes for harmony among the members, so

*that all the members care for each other
equally. If one part suffers, all the parts
suffer with it, and if one part is honored, all
the parts are glad" (1 Corinthians 12:12-13,
18-26).*

This picture of interdependence well
represents the critical nature of both unity and
uniqueness. Not everyone is supposed to be a
well-recognized mouth or hand. The less visible
parts are just as important for the maintenance
and health of the organism. When body organs
start attacking each other, the results are as
detrimental as an autoimmune disease or
cancer. Our focus has to continually return to
remaining in Christ, in His love.

After this passage Paul goes on to
describe the various spiritual gifts that make
individuals unique and important, then tells
what trumps the value of all of them: Love. I
picture love in the Body of Christ as the role
blood plays in the human body. It flows from
one part to the next, carrying the needed
oxygen and nutrients, and removing the left
over carbon dioxide and waste. It always
returns to the heart, where it is renewed,
cleansed, and pumped out again. No part of the
body can survive when it is cut off from the flow
of blood.

In the same way we are called to continue passing on God's love for each other, caring for each other, helping each other remain spiritually healthy, and valuing all parts of the Body for what roles God intended them to play. Toxic relationships can be cleansed and hurting individuals can find healing when receiving the love originating from Christ and His bloodshed. I know I find joy in passing on that love and seeing the powerful effects it can have.

I remember the unity and love I felt on our team in Kazakhstan being a reason to rejoice, and it was particularly through the difficult times that we grew closer. Yet I didn't fully appreciate it until coming back to the US and having trouble finding a similar degree of fellowship. In contrast to the team environment in Kazakhstan was my experience in Finland for a summer. It felt like a spiritually parched land. This was clearly evident in the city where I lived, as there was one single church that nobody, literally *nobody*, attended, except on Easter. The building was simply a display of architecture for tourists. While God was still present in my life, it was not the same without having the fellowship of other believers. I was very glad to find a church in the capital city, and I took the train to get there on Sundays. To worship God with people from a wide range of countries felt like water to a parched throat, a reason to rejoice.

The love of God is also the central theme of missions, hopefully love spilling over from within the church. Our calling is to introduce the grace of God to those who don't yet know Him, that they may join us in glorifying His name. It's not about a tally of how many people we see turn to God or how many new churches are formed, nor is it based purely on our strategic skills to touch every life we encounter. Those factors of strategy have some meaning and value for appropriate use of resources.

Ideally, on a daily basis our key motivation is being filled with the Presence of God to the point where we cannot help but joyfully share the overflowing love of God with others. He has perfect plans, and our job is to follow His guidance with the ultimate desire to glorify His name. The fulfillment of that desire comes both in the present reality and far past what our imaginations can predict for eternity.

After years of struggling with health issues, and never being sure of what might lie ahead, my desire deepened for my daily life to be in line with His purposes, filled with His love. How often I fall short or get distracted! Yet when returning to the right focus on God,

He graciously welcomes me back. Even in a career of helping others, I want to do so not purely for the self-satisfaction of feeling like I'm making a difference in the lives of others, but out of a desire to see God's name glorified. With that mindset, the same reason for finding joy in life remains constant even if unexpected factors come into play.

Conclusion

In summary, it is a privilege to enter God's Holy Presence, to come to His altar. Only through grace can we do so and we are invited to accept that abundant gift without questions of self-worth or the guilt of not having earned it. This privilege is a reason to rejoice, even in times of suffering, or perhaps especially in times of suffering. Such joy comes particularly as we share that gift of grace and love with others, both through mutual support within the Body of Christ and inviting others to join us. Paul prayed this for the Thessalonians:

> *"May the Lord make your love increase and overflow for each other and for everyone else, just as ours does for you. May he strengthen your hearts so that you will be blameless and holy in the presence of our God and Father when our Lord Jesus comes with all his holy ones"* *(1 Thessalonians 3:12-13).*

I am grateful that over the years of uncertainty and physical challenges, my Lord sustained me and shaped me, offering His own love in many ways and blessing me through others as well. It's been a long journey, just as it was for Israel in the desert, and it is my hope that the upcoming season will be one of passing on what God has taught me.

Even though I have no way of knowing what will happen in the future with my health or any other challenges that may come my way, I have the promise of ever being able to run into my Lord's Presence and receive His grace. I can trust in His strength in my weakness as I surrender myself to His Sovereignty. And I can participate in the Body of Christ as a vessel of His love, drawing not from my own resources, but overflowing from what God pours into me. Day by day, as I look back on these stones of remembrance, I want to rejoice as I live for God's glory.

"Praise be to the Lord, for he has heard my cry for mercy. The Lord is my strength and my shield; my heart trusts in him, and I am helped. My heart leaps for joy and I will give thanks to him in song" (Psalms 28:6-7).

Will you join me in this song?

Epilogue

T ime passed quickly after writing the initial draft of this book, soon after I graduated from college. I moved to Virginia and was rapidly immersed in a doctoral program, working toward my ongoing desire to become a psychologist and provide care for missionaries. With thousands of hours invested in academics, I put this project aside for the most part, occasionally opening the file and looking over it. Class by class, year after year, I got closer to finishing my doctorate in clinical psychology, often grateful that I was doing relatively well, with stable health and a goal in sight.

At certain points I realized that my newer friends and acquaintances met me at a very different place than those who had witnessed the changes and challenges over the years. This was a significant contrast to those I had met during times of utter weakness, when

I had likely left a memory that did not represent who I was before or after. Some of my physical struggles remained evident to friends early on in grad school; I still had to ask for rides to get groceries before I was able to get a driver's license, some witnessed a seizure occurred in the classroom building when attempting to reduce medication, and friends took me for my follow-up MRIs. But new acquaintances knew only as much as I disclosed; which usually was fairly limited early in a relationship. I did not want to be identified as "the sick one" (as I had in the past heard when being differentiated from other siblings).

Yet a change in perception of myself was likely more necessary for my own eyes than those of others. I still saw and felt the physical aftermath as I chose what clothes to wear and parted my hair to cover the long scar from surgery. Although I could readily encourage others to see their worth as God's creation, rather than value being based on the perception of others, I easily slipped into questioning what others might think of me. That struggle is one that does not easily dissipate; desiring approval is a subtle habit. Yet thinking back on the years past, or looking at the symbolic Rocks of Remembrance, can serve as a good reminder to look at this clay jar as a vessel, usable by God even if the outward appearance is marred.

Opportunities to become that vessel of comfort, or at times confrontation, came hand-in-hand with the clinical component of training. I saw many broken lives and relationships, while also having the chance to participate in the healing process. Some individuals were more ready for change than others, bringing varying degrees of joys and frustrations, times of apparent progress and other periods where I felt like I was floundering and did not know how to move forward. I had to learn to surrender my clients and their lives back to God; He is also Sovereign in their lives.

Despite challenges along the way, my desire to work in the field of mental health was confirmed, especially through short-term opportunities to integrate what I was learning into an international or missions-related context. Networking with others in the field of Member Care and trauma work in South Africa served as glimpses of the goal, providing hope I actually might reach it.

There were milestones: finishing my M.A., passing the comprehensive exams, being matched for an internship in a competitive system, and leaving for Missouri to start the internship. At each point I was acutely aware that I had reached that place only by the grace of God.

I found myself seizing opportunities as they came along, from doing trauma work in Chile after a devastating earthquake to authoring articles and book chapters. In part motivation came with an underlying awareness of the brevity of life, a reality reinforced by an annual MRI to check for any changes in scarred tissue of my brain. A different, subtle set of markers was also present: 5 years since brain surgery, seizures under control long enough to get a driver's license, and passing the median length of survival for individuals with low-grade astrocytomas. I appreciated being alive and moving forward.

Milestones evolved into end points: defending and printing my dissertation, finishing my internship, graduation with a doctorate, and completion of requirements for licensure as clinical psychologist. These ran parallel to new beginnings, being accepted for a position doing Member Care for a year in Kenya, officially opening a micro-publishing company, and taking part in the creation of an academic journal for research on cross-cultural families.

I am frequently amazed at all God has orchestrated as part of my life thus far. While my view of the future is very clouded, I have hope in His perfect plans, even though I know they will include times of trial. There is hope in knowing my final destination, enjoying the glory and love of God for eternity.

To contact Emily Hervey write to:

hervey@worldwidefamilies.org